# JOYRIDE!

Dee Phillips

WITHDRAWN
FROM STOCK

**READZ NE**

53 26 484

# READZONE BOOKS

First published in this edition 2013

**ReadZone Books Limited**
**50 Godfrey Avenue**
**Twickenham**
**TW2 7PF**
**UK**

All rights reserved. No part of this publication may be reproduced, stored in a retrieval system, or transmitted, in any form, or by any means, electronic, mechanical, photocopying, or otherwise, without the prior permission of ReadZone Books Limited

© **Copyright Ruby Tuesday Books Limited 2009**

© **Copyright in this edition ReadZone Books 2013**

The right of the Author to be identified as the Author of this work has been asserted by the Author in accordance with the Copyright, Designs and Patents Act 1988

Every attempt has been made by the Publisher to secure appropriate permissions for material reproduced in this book. If there has been any oversight we will be happy to rectify the situation in future editions or reprints. Written submissions should be made to the Publishers.

British Library Cataloguing in Publication Data (CIP) is available for this title.

ISBN 9781783220007

Printed in Malta by Melita Press

*Developed and Created by* Ruby Tuesday Books Ltd
**Project Director** – Ruth Owen
**Consultant** – Lorraine Petersen

Images courtesy of Shutterstock

### ACKNOWLEDGEMENTS

With thanks to Lorraine Petersen, Chief Executive of NASEN, for her help in the development and creation of these books

**Visit our website: www.readzonebooks.com**

Dan, Jess, Sam and I.
The red car.
"Look," says Dan. "The keys are inside!"

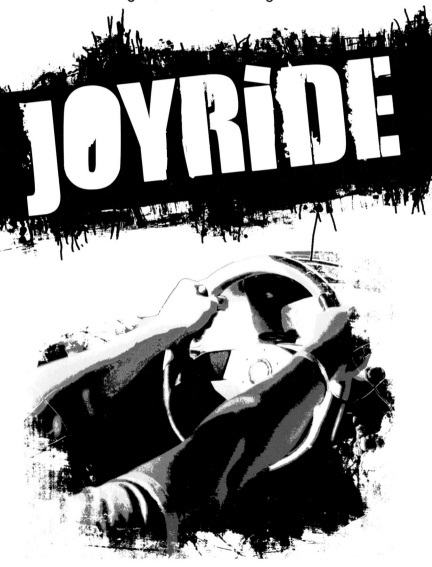

# JOYRIDE

**ONE MOMENT CAN CHANGE YOUR LIFE FOREVER**

4

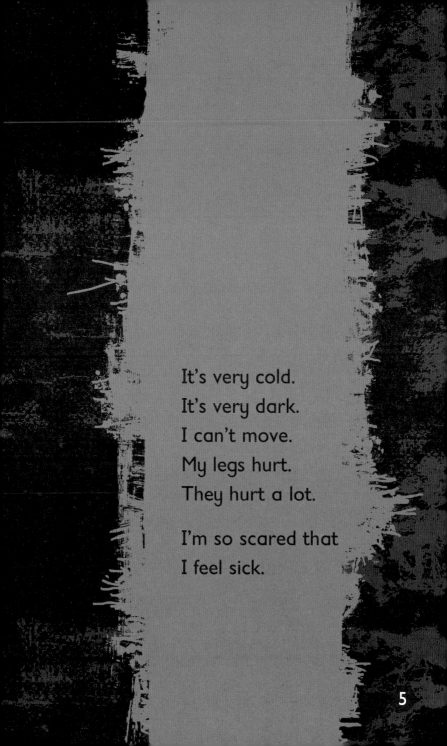

It's very cold.
It's very dark.
I can't move.
My legs hurt.
They hurt a lot.

I'm so scared that
I feel sick.

I can smell something.
Oh my God!
I can smell petrol.
Why can I smell petrol?
Why can't I move?

I'M SO
SCARED...

...I'M GOING TO BE SICK!

I can see dark sky above me.
Dark sky and dark trees.
Where are we?
What happened?

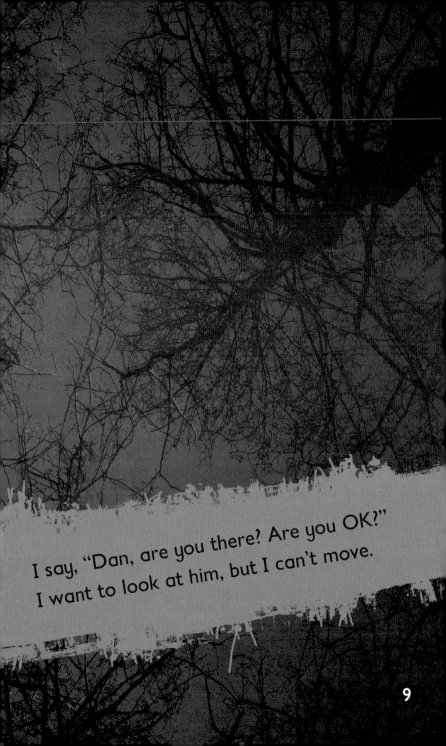

I say, "Dan, are you there? Are you OK?"
I want to look at him, but I can't move.

I can hear Sam crying.
I want to look at her, but I can't move.
I say, "It's OK, Sam."
But she doesn't stop crying.

God. It's so cold.
So cold and dark.
I can't move.
I can't hear anything.
Just Sam crying.

IT'S OK, SAM.
IT'S OK.

Sam wasn't crying ten minutes ago.
She was laughing.
We were all laughing.
Dan, Jess, Sam and I.

We were all messing around and laughing.

Then Dan saw the car.
The red car.

Dan loves cars.
Dan has loved cars since
we were little kids.

"Look," said Dan. "The keys are inside!"
He opened the driver's door of the car.

Dan is crazy like that.
You never know what he will do next.

Dan got into the driver's seat.
I opened the passenger door.
Dan said, "Want to go for a drive, Andy?"
That's just like Dan!
He's been doing crazy stuff since
we were little kids.

Sam and I got in the back of the car.
Jess got in the front next to Dan.
I put my arm around Sam. It felt good.
Sam was holding me tight.
She was laughing, but she was scared.

Dan turned the key.
The car started.

WE WERE ALL LAUGHING.

21

The car started to move.

Ten miles an hour.

Thirty miles an hour.

Fifty miles an hour.

We were all laughing, but we were scared.

Dan yelled, "I'm a good driver!"

Seventy miles an hour.

Ninety miles an hour.

Then Dan hit a kerb!

 Like a bomb.

Suddenly, the car was flying through the air.

Jess was screaming.

Sam was screaming, too.

FLYING

SCREAMING

The car flew through the air.
Then there was a noise like the
end of everything!

It's very cold.
I can't move.
My legs hurt a lot.
I'm so scared.

Now there are lights.

Flashing lights.

I want to cry.
I feel like a little kid.
A scared little kid.
I want to hold Sam's hand,
but I can't move.
I say, "It's OK, Sam.
The police are here."

A light shines in my face.
A man says, "It's OK, son. Hold on."
I like his voice. He sounds like my dad.

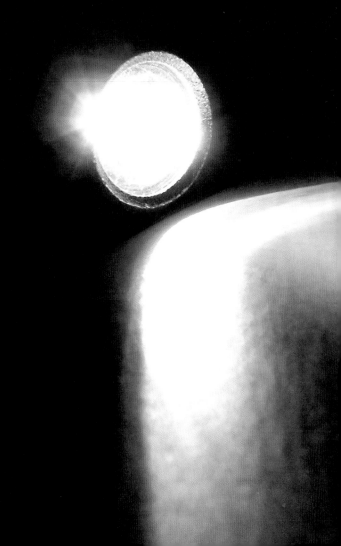

Another light shines into the car.
A woman says, "The girl is OK, too, Sir."

# WE ARE IN BIG TROUBLE.

But the police sound OK.
I'm not so scared now.

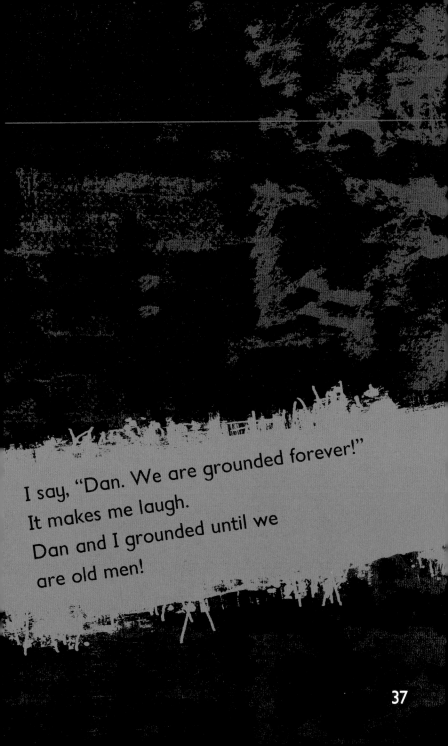

I say, "Dan. We are grounded forever!"
It makes me laugh.
Dan and I grounded until we
are old men!

A light shines on
the front of the car.
It shines through
cracked glass.

The woman says, "What about the two in the front, Sir?"

I hear the man's voice.
The man who sounds like my dad.

He says, "It's too late. There's
nothing we can do for them."

It's very cold.

I can't move.

Everything hurts.

# I'M GOING TO BE SICK...

## BEST FRIENDS
### ON YOUR OWN

Makes everyone laugh

DANGER

*Who is Dan?*

Hip-hop music

Cool
Funny
Lots of friends
Risky
Show-off
Thief

SPEED

loves cars

Make a collage of words and pictures about Dan or Andy. Look for clues in the book and imagine:

- What things they like.
- What they like doing.
- What their friends think they are like.
- What they are really like.

## WHAT IF?
### WITH A PARTNER

Dan and Andy met when they were kids. Andy knows Dan is crazy but he still gets into the car! Discuss:

- Why did Andy get in?
- What might have happened if Andy hadn't got in? What might Dan have said?

# FREEZE IT!
## IN A GROUP

Read and discuss pages 20 to 23.

- Plan a role-play and act it out for a friend.

- Act it out a second time. This time, ask your friend to shout 'Freeze!' at some point.

- What is each character thinking and feeling at this point?

# NEWS REPORT
## ON YOUR OWN / WITH A PARTNER / IN A GROUP

Make a newspaper, radio or TV report about the crash. Think about:

- The facts – where it took place, how fast the car was going, the type of car…

- What did Andy and Sam say about the crash?

- What did other people, such as the police or the friends' parents, say about the crash?

TEEN TRAGEDY

IF YOU ENJOYED
THIS BOOK,
TRY THESE OTHER
**RIGHT NOW!**
BOOKS.

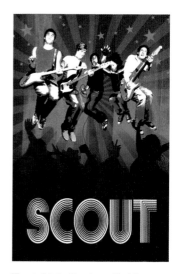

Tonight is the band's big chance. Tonight, a record company scout is at their gig!

Tonight, Vicky must make a choice. Stay in London with her boyfriend Chris. Or start a new life in Australia.

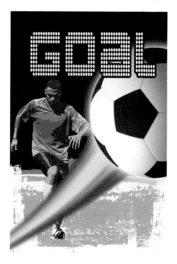

Today is Carl's trial with City. There's just one place up for grabs. But today, everything is going wrong!

It's Saturday night.
Two angry guys. Two knives.
There's going to be a fight.

Sophie hates this new town.
She misses her friends.
There's nowhere to skate!

Ed's platoon is under attack.
Another soldier is in danger.
Ed must risk his own life to
save him.

It's just an old, empty house.
Lauren must spend the night
inside. Just Lauren and the
ghost...